Six
STEPS TO
CLARIFY YOUR
CALLING

Six STEPS TO CLARIFY YOUR CALLING

Carol Kent & Karen Lee-Thorp

NavPress

BRINGING TRUTH TO LIFE

P.O. Box 35001, Colorado Springs, Colorado 80935

OUR GUARANTEE TO YOU

We believe so strongly in the message of our books that we are making this quality guarantee to you. If for any reason you are disappointed with the content of this book, return the title page to us with your name and address and we will refund to you the list price of the book. To help us serve you better, please briefly describe why you were disappointed. Mail your refund request to: NavPress, P.O. Box 35002, Colorado Springs, CO 80935.

The Navigators is an international Christian organization. Our mission is to reach, disciple, and equip people to know Christ and to make Him known through successive generations. We envision multitudes of diverse people in the United States and every other nation who have a passionate love for Christ, live a lifestyle of sharing Christ's love, and multiply spiritual laborers among those without Christ.

NavPress is the publishing ministry of The Navigators. NavPress publications help believers learn biblical truth and apply what they learn to their lives and ministries. Our mission is to stimulate spiritual formation among our readers.

ISBN 1-57683-203-1

Cover photo by Colin Hawkins / Tony Stone
Cover design by Jennifer Mahalik
Creative Team: Amy Spencer, Terry Behimer, Tim Howard, Heather Nordyke

Some of the anecdotal illustrations in this book are true to life and are included with the permission of the persons involved. All other illustrations are composites of real situations, and any resemblance to people living or dead is coincidental.

Unless otherwise identified, all Scripture quotations in this publication are taken from the *HOLY BIBLE: NEW INTERNATIONAL VERSION®* (NIV®). Copyright © 1973, 1978, 1984 by International Bible Society. Used by permission of Zondervan Publishing House. All rights reserved. Other version used: the *King James Version* (KJV).

Printed in the United States of America

2 3 4 5 6 7 8 9 10 11 12 13 14 15 / 05 04 03 02

CONTENTS

INTRODUCTION

God Calling

SURE, some people just want Jesus as fire insurance. But most of us know God is embarked on a great work in the world, and we want to participate. We want to know that our lives count for something. When we read of how God called the great prophets, the apostles, and the evangelists to mighty works, we dream of being called to something too.

The Bible has a lot to say about our calling as Christians. Most of it has to do with our *general* calling, the life to which God calls everyone who will respond to Him. "There is one body and one Spirit—just as you were called to one hope when you were called . . . " (Ephesians 4:4). But when most people today wonder about their calling, they are thinking about their *specific* calling, what God is asking of them in particular.

We want to know we're unique and special. We need to know that the good Shepherd "calls his own sheep by name" (John 10:3), each of us by our unique name. Yet sometimes we imagine that all true callings come in dramatic visions, like those given to Paul and Isaiah. We tune out God's quiet voice speaking to us through the Scriptures and the ordinariness of life.

This study offers you the chance to take some time to listen to that voice. It's not likely that after six sessions you'll be one hundred percent certain of God's map for the rest of your life, but it's very likely you'll gain some clarity about a next step. You'll consider what it means to follow Jesus, examine things in your life that hinder you from discerning and responding to God's call, learn from the ways Jesus and His disciples handled their calls, and explore some of God's big dreams and purposes. You'll also reflect on who you are—your dreams, passions, qualities, and strengths—as you work toward constructing a purpose statement that expresses what your life is about. And you'll practice habits of listening for God's guidance—habits that will continue to be valuable as you move forward.

Receiving a call from God won't make you more important or provide proof of God's love. But responding to God's whisper will give your life a sense of focus and meaning that material success or the world's applause can't begin to match.

God is calling. Is your line busy?

HOW TO USE THIS GUIDE

You were born to be a woman of influence. No—we don't mean a busybody or a queen bee, telling others what to do or making their lives revolve around yours. You were born to model your life on Jesus' life, and in so doing, be a model for others. Perhaps your influence will happen in a few quiet words over coffee, in a hug or a prayer. Don't say, "Not me—I'm barely treading water!" If you have the Spirit of God in your life, you have what it takes. God wants to influence people through you.

We've created these *Designed for Influence* Bible studies to draw out this loving, serving, celebrating side of you. You can use this study guide in your private time with God, but you'll gain even more from it if you meet with a small group of other women who share your desire to grow and give. The study is designed around the seven life-changing principles explored in Carol Kent's book, *Becoming a Woman of Influence*. These principles, which underlay Jesus' style of influencing others, are:

- Time alone with God
- Walking and talking
- Storytelling
- Asking questions
- Compassion
- Unconditional love
- Casting vision

Each of the six sessions in this guide contains these seven sections:

An Opening Story. When you see the word "I" in this guide, you're hearing from Carol. She begins each session with a story from her own life to let you know we're not making this stuff up in some spiritual hothouse; we care about these issues because we're living them. As you read these stories, look for a point of connection between your life and Carol's.

Connecting. Next comes your chance to tell your own story about the topic at hand. If you're studying on your own, take a few minutes to write down a piece of your life story in response to the questions in this section. If you're meeting with a group, tell your stories to each other. Nothing brings a group of women together like sharing stories. It's not necessary for each person to answer every question in the rest of the study, but each person should have a chance to respond to the "Connecting" questions. Sharing stories is great fun, but try to keep your answers brief so that you'll have time for the rest of the study!

Learning from the Master. The entire Bible is the Word of God. Yet Jesus Himself is the Word of God made flesh. The Bible studies in this series focus on Jesus' words and actions in the Gospels. You'll get to see how Jesus Himself grappled with situations much like those you face. He's the smartest guy in history, the closest to the Father, the one who understood life better than anyone else. This is your opportunity to follow Him around and watch how He did it. If you're meeting with a group, you don't need to answer the questions ahead of time, but it would be helpful to read through them and begin thinking about them. When your group gathers, ask for one or more volunteers to read the Scripture aloud. If the story is lengthy, you could take turns reading paragraphs. Or if you really want to have fun, assign the roles of Jesus and the other characters to different readers. Karen wrote the Bible study section of this guide, and if you have any questions or comments, you can e-mail her at bible.study@navpress.com.

A Reflection. This section contains some thoughts on the topic, as well as some questions that invite you to apply what you've learned to your own life. If you're meeting with a group, it is helpful, but not necessary, to read the reflection ahead of time. When your group reaches this point in the study, you can allow people a few minutes to read over the reflection to refresh their memories. Talk about the ideas in this section that seem especially helpful to you.

Talking with God. This section closes your meeting if you're studying with a group. Inviting God to enable you to live what you've discussed may be the most important thing you do together. In addition to the prayer ideas suggested in this section, feel free to include your personal concerns.

Time Alone with God. This section and the next are your "homework" if you are meeting with a group. The first part of your "homework" is to take some time during the week to be with God. In this section you'll find ideas for prayer, journaling, thinking, or just *being* with God. If you're already accustomed to taking time away from the rush of life to reflect and pray, then you know how these quiet moments energize you for the rest of your week. If you've believed yourself to be "too busy" to take this time to nourish your hungry soul, then this is your chance to taste the feast God has prepared for you.

Walking with Others. The second part of your "homework" is to pass on God's love to someone else in some way. Here you'll sample what it means to be a woman of influence simply by giving away something you've received. This is your chance to practice compassion, unconditional love, and vision-casting with the women you encounter in your daily life.

That's how the Christian life works: we draw apart to be with God, then we go back into the world to love as we have been loved.

If you're meeting with a group, one woman will need to take responsibility for facilitating the discussion at each meeting. You can rotate this responsibility or let the same person facilitate all six sessions. The facilitator's main task is to keep the discussion moving forward and to make sure everyone has a chance to speak. This will be easiest if you limit the size of your discussion group to no more than eight people. If your group is larger than eight (especially in a Sunday school class), consider dividing into subgroups of four to six people for your discussion.

Spiritual influence is not just for super-Christians. You can make a difference in someone's life by letting God work through you. Take a chance—the results may surprise you!

1

FOLLOW ME

God calls you and says, Look. This is a need.
*You see the need, you know you can fill the need —
and deep in your heart you know your life will never
be the same.*

—PAM FARREL[1]

TEARS poured down my cheeks and I felt pinned to the back of my seat in the auditorium. It was a Winning Women Retreat weekend. There were almost three thousand women in the audience, and we were there for a variety of reasons. Some were looking for spiritual meaning in their lives. Others left husbands babysitting young children and were enjoying a weekend away with good friends. A few had no idea it was a conference based on learning biblical truth. I had attended this event once before and had looked forward to the great speakers and inspirational music.

I had been teaching drama, speech, and English to junior-high students that year — my very first year to sign a contract and commit to the beginning of what I believed would be a lifetime career in education. The fall retreat was a chance for me to get away for the weekend with friends and listen to God's voice to me through the speakers and musicians. I was in my early twenties and had a heart to know the mind of God. I believed in the direction He was leading and loved the opportunity to influence the minds and hearts of students. Before the conference even started, I told God I was open to hear what He wanted to say to me.

Halfway through the weekend, I was seated in the back of the main floor of the auditorium. Jill Briscoe was the Bible teacher during that hour, and her crisp English accent held my attention. But more than that, her command of the Word of God was riveting. There was an authority in her voice as she read from the Bible and applied biblical truth to everyday situations.

I can't tell you where the passage was located or even what the theme of the message was. But God spoke to me. He asked me to follow Him. It wasn't an audible voice, and no one around me seemed particularly moved emotionally, but His gentle Spirit enveloped me and I knew He was speaking to my heart. He was asking me to get ready to serve Him through teaching and speaking about His Word. As I sat there, I knew He was asking me to permeate my mind with the study of the Bible so I would have something of substance to say when He opened doors for me to speak or teach. I had a degree in speech education and was working on a master's degree in communication arts. I was trained to be an educator and had never dreamed of using this gift outside the classroom.

But there was no mistaking His call. As I sat riveted to the seat near the back of that auditorium, I knew He was waiting for my answer. And I said, *Yes!* Someone observing me might have noticed I was moved by the message of the hour, but they could not have known how my response to God's call would change my life. It was the beginning of a lifelong quest to listen to His voice, observe what He was doing, and join Him by using my God-given gifts to further His kingdom wherever He called me to go. In this session we'll look at how Jesus called His first disciples, and we'll see what we can learn about our own callings.

1. Who is one of your heroes? Name someone, living or dead, whom you admire very much. (For the purpose of this discussion, exclude people in the Bible.)

During the past century, the word "calling" has come to be used interchangeably with "career." In our money-oriented culture, we think of our calling as the work we do for money. However, the two are not the same. When Jesus called His first disciples, He was calling them to much more than a career.

2. Read the following stories of Jesus calling His disciples. In each case, what does Jesus call them to do? What do the called ones do?

Matthew 4:18-22

Matthew 9:9-13

John 1:35-46

3. Over and over, Jesus said, "Follow me." What did this call involve for these disciples? From these passages and anything you know about the rest of the New Testament, what did following Jesus actually mean on a day-by-day basis?

4. Imagine being Matthew the tax collector. You have a secure, not too strenuous, well-paying job. If you are sitting at a tax booth, then you are probably an

under-collector employed by a chief tax collector. If you walk away from your tax booth in the middle of a work-day, you can forget coming back. What risks are you taking if you get up and walk away with Jesus? What will happen if you're wrong about Jesus?

5. Read Matthew 16:24-26. In this passage, what elements does Jesus add to the calling of a disciple that further explain what it means to "Follow me"?

To one of his parishioners who was struggling with this notion of following Jesus, Pastor Jan Hettinga said, "Dan, *believing* is a spectator sport. *Following* is what makes you a player. Following is where the cost of commitment shows up, and that never gets any easier. According to Jesus, there's something of the cross in it. A cross that must be taken up daily as we follow Him. The cross always means 'not my will but thine be done.' It means submission to our Lord's leadership of our lives, and that always means dying to self-in-control."

Dan went home and prayed hard. He thought he heard God speaking to him in his heart: "He asked me why I didn't trust Him. The moment I became aware of the question I knew I was focusing on the right issue. For the first time in my life I was able to admit that I've been holding out on following Christ because I might not like where He'll lead me. I know it sounds arrogant, but something in me would rather trust myself than God."[2]

6. What do you think about Dan, who would rather trust himself than God? How are you like or unlike him?

7. Following Jesus means denying ourselves (that is, subordinating our agendas to God's), taking up a cross (that is, risking death), and giving up efforts to save our lives (that is, giving up our strategies to get our needs met). Why would anybody follow a leader who calls her to such risks?

8. The most basic calling every Christian gets is like a blank check: "Follow me." If we don't trust the One Who Calls enough to do this daily, we can't expect to get more specific instructions. When (if ever) have you been aware of Jesus' call, "Follow me"? How have you responded?

Learning to Follow His Voice

As a person who enjoys dramatic moments, definite direction, and a specific plan for my future, I've always wished that God would speak to me through neon lights in the sky, an audible voice, or a supernatural experience. However, that's not how I've learned to follow His call. I most often hear His voice when I embrace the following facts:

- *God has a plan for my life that will maximize the use of my gifts for His kingdom.* David Frahm says, "God has made each of us His representative steward, assigned to some tailored role in 'tending His garden.' We know that God has the whole world in His hands, certainly— but the question to ask is, What part of it has He assigned to your care?"[3]
- *God reveals His call on my life after I confess all sin in my heart, verbalize my openness to His plan for my life, and make my life available for His direction.* A wonderful way to express this response is through a prayer written by the authors of *Experiencing God:* "Lord, I will do anything that Your kingdom requires of me. Wherever You want me to be, I'll go. Whatever the circumstances, I'm willing to follow. If You want to meet a need through my life, I am Your servant; and I will do whatever is required."[4]
- *God's call on my life will be confirmed through His Word and through His Spirit.* Dee Brestin reminds us that God's tender call is always confirmed through Scripture: "The primary way God speaks to us is through His Word. Sometimes He speaks through the nudge of His Spirit, but we need to check those nudges against His Word—for His Spirit never leads against His Word."[5]

- *God often affirms His call through the affirmation of people who are close to Him.* Within a few months of the call God gave me to study His Word and teach His truth to women, I had several seasoned Christian women come up to me after a Bible class and say, "You have a real gift for teaching the Bible." It was as if I could hear God's voice from heaven saying, "Go, girl! You are following Me in the right direction."

- *God's call always involves a cost — being willing to die to my own plans and selfish desires.* Christina DiStefano Davis, author of *Totally Surrounded,* tells of God's call on her young life to bring the gospel to people in the jungles of the Philippines. One day she wrote in her journal, "If my life were my own, I would be doing what was comfortable and fun. When I gave my life to Christ, I made a decision to lose my life to find it in Him. My priorities were no longer my own, but His."[6]

9. Where are you in the process of discerning God's current call on your life? Consider the five points just listed. Are you in the place of needing to believe God does have a plan for your life? Are you in the place of needing to make yourself available?

Take five minutes of silence to reflect on the call, "Follow me." Close your eyes and listen to the group leader say, "Jesus' call to us is 'Follow me.'" Let the words "Follow me" roll around in your mind. You can write a prayer back to God in response to these words, or you can just sit with your eyes closed and listen. Let the presence of God come among you as you sit together, listening to His quiet call. At the end of five minutes, the leader can pray aloud briefly. Then invite people to share what came to them during the silence. If you'd like, you can close with the prayer from *Experiencing God* quoted on page 21.

Continue to meditate on the call, "Follow me." Ask God to show you what it means for you to follow Jesus in your daily life at work, in relationships, and in the wider community to which you belong. Where is Jesus in your world? How can you follow Him in what He is already doing? Write notes of any thoughts that come to you on this subject.

Sooner or later, the call to follow Jesus leads us into other people's lives, where Jesus is already at work. Some of us are only too eager to give others advice about how they should follow Jesus. But some of us get caught up in our own concerns or we doubt that we have anything to offer others. To all of us, Jesus says, "Follow me into the life of this daughter of mine. Don't rush ahead of me. Don't try to take over my job. But listen to me, and I will give you ways to encourage her growth."

This week, look around you for a woman in your life who is younger or newer to faith than you. You don't have to "teach" that person or commit to "mentoring" her for years. Just agree with God that you're available to be present for that woman, to encourage her, to be whatever God would like you to be in her life for this season. *This season* might be a single contact with a stranger, or a friendship of a few weeks or months. It might grow into a long-term friendship. You're not on the hook forever; just agree with God to be available, and ask God what's needed.

If you're new to faith yourself, maybe you know someone else in the same boat. You may not be able to offer deep wisdom about God (yet), but you can share your thirst to know God. Make yourself available as a comrade in the enterprise of discovering God together.

> *Answering the call is the way to find and fulfill the central purpose of your life.*
>
> —OS GUINNESS[7]

2

TUNE OUT THE COMPETITION

Listen to God's whisper saying to you, You have a
purpose and I have a plan. *As you follow His
leading toward that vision of what you were created
to become . . . you will know that God loves you,
that He has a plan for you, that He wants to give
you abundant life—peace, joy, and purpose in the
midst of chaos.*

—SHEILA WEST [1]

IT was my senior year of high school. Decisions. Financial issues.
Life's work. Falling in love. Higher education. Choices.

I believed the best way I could follow His call on my life was
to get more education at a Christian university, but there were other
things pulling at me. The most intense competition was a naval offi-
cer whose parents attended my father's church. He was four years
older than I, and he swept me off my feet with his fun-loving personality and his stories of international travel and intrigue. His

sparkling blue eyes, curly eyelashes, and dimpled grin added fuel to the fire in my heart.

Bill had completed one tour of duty on the U.S.S. Enterprise, and now he was headed to the East Coast for a "mainland" assignment. I often envisioned him in his dress whites meeting me at the end of the center aisle of the church on our wedding day. In the spring of my final year of high school, he was home on leave. We had a wonderful time together. I loved his family. I liked his personality. I thought he was drop-dead gorgeous. I wished he was a little closer to the Lord, but I was sure he would "come around." The night before he left for his new assignment, he asked me to marry him.

The tug in my heart was heavy. I thought I loved Bill enough to spend the rest of my life with him, but I was also convinced that God had a purpose for my life—perhaps as a teacher or a missionary—and that meant I needed more education. I soon knew Bill was unwilling to wait and would break off the relationship if I didn't marry him right after graduation. I had been accepted at two schools, but I was so in love. How could I turn my back on this man? As I asked God for guidance, I did three specific things: (1) I kept reading the Bible consistently, daily; (2) I sought the counsel of mature Christians who knew me well; and (3) I asked God to help me recognize His will and His purpose for my life.

The next day I was having my devotions and my eyes fell on these verses: "The word of the Lord came to me: *Son of man, set your face toward the south...*" (Ezekiel 20:45-46, emphasis added). One of the two schools I was considering was in the South. I had received strong recommendations from several people

I respected that I would fit well in this setting. Then a wonderful older Christian came to our home to discuss his concerns over my interest in "the young sailor." He knew my heart was fixed on following Jesus completely, and he was not at all convinced that the young man I thought I loved had the same passion for Christ.

While taking one verse on turning my face toward the south would never have been my *only* way to discern the will of God, when I realized the Scripture came out of my daily reading, and it lined up completely with the affirmations and warnings from Christians I trusted, I knew what I had to do. I could not be distracted by the temptation to marry this man when my heart's true home was at peace in following God's call to the school in the South. Many things can distract us and tempt us not to hear His call. In this session we'll look at what hindered one man from heeding Jesus' call.

1. What is one thing you would *hate* for God to call you to be or do? What would be your worst nightmare of a calling?

"Follow me" is the call to all Christians. However, unless the One Who Calls is our heart's true home and the object of our deepest desire, secondary things will distract us from following His call.

2. Read Mark 10:17-22. What positive qualities do you observe in the man who approached Jesus here?

3. What hindered this man from heeding Jesus' call, "Follow me"?

In response to the man's question about eternal life, Jesus pointed him to five of the Ten Commandments. He omitted the four commandments about putting God first in all things and the commandment about coveting. (You could compare Mark 10:19 to Exodus 20:1-17.)

4. Do you think the man could have honestly said he had kept the commandments to put God first? What makes you say that?

5. Jesus didn't require every follower to give away all of his or her possessions. Why do you suppose His call to this particular man included that requirement?

Anything that feels like a source of life to us can become a distraction from God's call. Such things can be obviously destructive, like drugs, or they can be wonderful—a husband, children, a beautiful home, a successful career, a ministry that brings us respect. If any of those things is the source of our happiness, if we would doubt God's goodness if He asked us to let go of it, then it can close our ears to God's call. We cannot heed a new call if we are unwilling to accept the losses that come with change. Nor can we heed God's call if His voice is drowned out by the voices of people who seem more important to us. When we can rest in the knowledge that God is completely good and sufficient for all our needs, then we don't need to fear that He might call us to something that would make us miserable.

6. What are the things in your life that distract you from listening intently to hear God's call?

7. Do you worry at all that God might call you to something you would hate? If so, what are your concerns?

Tuning Out Distractions—Tuning in to God
How is it possible to live a "normal" life and tune out the distractions that compete with our relationship with God and our willingness to follow His leading? I've discovered a few principles that have helped me find my heart's true home in Him and stay focused on my purpose.

- *Read the Bible every day*—whether you feel like it or not, whether it's convenient or not, whether you think you can concentrate or not. The Bible is God's voice to us today. Dee Brestin says, "The most common way God speaks to us today is through His Word."[2] It's helpful to read systematically and with a question in mind. For instance, for the next month you could commit to reading one chapter of Matthew's gospel each day, asking, "What does this reveal about God's priorities?" A sense of God's call may emerge from a deeper understanding of His purposes in the world.
- *Respond to what you just read.* Write out two or three sentences that reflect what you believe God is saying to you through the Scripture you read.
- *Recognize and deal with distractions.* Does the person, situation, or event you are encountering draw you closer

to God or pull you away from Him? Is this person or situation a witnessing opportunity, or is this individual or situation likely to drag you down to a place where you will be drawn away from your spiritual purpose?

• *Repossess your passion for God's best.* Be single-minded, and seek His anointing on your life and ministry. Pamela Muse explains: "Anointing is when you are keeping pace with God. There is a wonderful era in your life when you've been through all the heartache and He's prepared you for your calling. All the machinery is working and the Holy Spirit is using you as a vessel. You're in step with the Lord, and there's an anointing that comes with that."[3]

For me, the best way to tune out distractions is to tune in to Him with "dove's eyes." Doves have single vision; their eyes do not rotate in the sockets. They can see only one thing at a time. Solomon understood the importance of single vision when he spoke to the Shulammite woman and said, "My dove in the clefts of the rock, in the hiding places on the mountainside, show me your face, let me hear your voice; for your voice is sweet, and your face is lovely" (Song of Songs 2:14). When we have single vision for Him, the distractions disappear, our focus is clear, and our purpose becomes visible.

8. What goes on inside you when you think about these ways of tuning out distractions? (For instance, do any of them make you say, *Yes!* Do any make you feel barriers going up inside?)

Perhaps the most profound thing we can say about being "on purpose" is that when that is our status, our condition, and our comfort, we find our lives have meaning, and when we are "off purpose," we are confused about meanings and motives.

—DUDLEY LYNCH AND PAUL K. KORDIS[4]

Give everyone a chance to finish this sentence in a prayer: "Lord, I think one thing that distracts me from hearing and answering your call is . . . " Let people think about this for a minute before you begin praying so they're not groping for words while others are praying.

When everyone has had an opportunity to pray, allow an open time for people to praise God for His goodness, for being more dear to your hearts than all the things that can distract you from Him.

It's easier to tune out distractions when our thoughts are captivated by the beauty and goodness of God. Look up Psalm 27:4 and read the verse aloud. Read it again slowly, listening to the meaning of each word. Choose a phrase that your heart needs to absorb more fully, such as "the beauty of the LORD." Close your eyes and let the phrase roll around in your mind. What is God saying to you here? Breathe the phrase in. As you breathe out, relax into the phrase. Let the Spirit of God wrap you in the truth of this verse.

Not all callings encompass the whole of our lives. God may be calling you to touch the life of another woman this week. Watch and listen for who that might be. How can you encourage her? Take a moment and ask her how you can pray for her.

> *Passion will carry you to your high place. It is when you are there, in the place of your passion, that you can say, I know who I was born to be.*
>
> —PAM FARREL[5]

3

PLAY TO AN AUDIENCE OF ONE

A life lived listening to the decisive call of God is a life lived before one audience that trumps all others — the Audience of One.

—OS GUINNESS[1]

FROM the time I was a little girl, I've always enjoyed pleasing people. Because my father was a minister, we frequently had out-of-town speakers or people from the congregation in for dinner or dessert, and I became the chief hostess and entertainer. After serving the company in the dining room, I would play the piano or sing with my sisters in the living room.

However, what appeared to be a good thing turned me into an adult who had a fear of losing control. I loved doing things well so there would never be cause for criticism. If everything and everybody connected with my family "looked" good, I was comfortable. However, when the appearances of the people around me were less than perfect, or when I let myself down by not living up to my own expectations, I felt agitated. I equated "following God's call" with "doing things perfectly." This behavior often turned me into a mean mother and a nagging wife.

When our son became a teenager, he had very different tastes in decorating from mine. One day when I walked into his room, I was appalled to see posters of popular musicians all over his meticulously painted walls. He had rearranged his furniture in an unsightly fashion, and he had dangled Army camouflage clothing and gear all around the room as a major part of his decor. I exploded. Breaking out in an agitated sweat, I angrily yelled, "Jason Paul Kent, you have made a *mess* of this room! I worked for weeks on getting you a bedspread that would perfectly match the draperies and the wall treatment, and you have turned this place into a disaster zone. How can we ever let anyone stay in the guest room down the hall again when they would have to walk past *your* room to get there? I can't believe you did this!"

Walking away, I knew I had wounded his spirit. My conscience bothered me for the rest of the evening. The posters on his walls weren't evil or inappropriate; they just didn't match the colors in the room and they violated my "decorating comfort zone." Jason stayed in his room. Pulling out my journal, I began to write out a prayer of confession:

> Lord, I blew it today. I don't need to tell you how
> badly I reacted. I was wrong and I need to apologize
> to you and to my son and ask for your forgiveness.
> But Lord, I know my outburst today is a symptom of
> a problem I've had for a long time. Almost everything

I do for you and for others has somehow been connected with my need to impress people. I've longed
for their approval, and I've wanted others to think
I'm a wonderful Christian wife and mother. I thought
if my house looked good enough and if my child was
a model of perfection, we'd all give You a better repu-
tation. But today I know I've been living my life to
please people, not to please You. Help me to change
and to live my life as if *You* are my only audience. If I
get *that* right, I'll treat my family right and I'll live
out my purpose.

I knocked on Jason's door. To my surprise, he let me in without any defensive words. I sat down on his bed and told him I had
been wrong. "I've been making issues about things that don't matter. Actually, your room looks just like a teenager's room *should* look.
Will you forgive me for my bad attitude? I've already told God I
want to quit being a people-pleaser and start being a God-pleaser."
He hugged me and said he had already forgiven me.

Each of us has our own temptations to seek approval, whether
through success, beauty, or saving souls. We all need to ask, Am I
living out my "purpose" so others will be impressed with me, or am
I living for the pleasure of the One who created me? In this session
we'll look at how Jesus played to an Audience of One even when
His life was on the line.

1. When you were a child, who did you try to please?
   (Your parents? Your teachers? An older sibling? Yourself?)
   How did you go about that?

Jesus was constantly under pressure to play to the crowd. He infuriated the people in His hometown by telling them what they didn't want to hear (Luke 4:14-30). But Jesus had an Audience of One, the One He called "him who sent me" (John 6:38). His conviction that He had been both called and sent gave His life incredible focus.

2. How does Jesus define His calling in these passages?

   John 6:38

   John 7:18

   John 8:28-29

3. How would you compare your own sense of calling to what you've just read?

Jesus could have been a huge celebrity, but He threw it all away. John 18:28–19:11 describes Jesus' trial before the Roman governor, Pontius Pilate. Pilate was the one official in Jerusalem who had the legal right to condemn Jesus to death or set Him free. If Jesus had played to please the governor, He might have saved His life.

4. Read John 18:28–19:11. What words and actions of Jesus show that He was acting to please His Father alone?

5. Pilate couldn't believe it. Look at 19:10. Why did Pilate think any sane person would try to please him?

6. Look at 19:11. What did Pilate not understand? Why did it make sense to play to an Audience of One?

7. There's nothing wrong with trying to make people happy when it fits with God's command to love. However, have you ever had to choose between pleasing people and pleasing your true Audience? If so, what was the choice?

Becoming Inner-Directed Instead of Other-Directed

One of the great freedoms of my adult life has been accepting the fact that the only thing that's really important is what God thinks of me. If I live every day knowing what matters most is my love relationship with Him — simply being in His presence, delighting in His company, understanding His character — everything else falls into its proper place. Out of the pleasure of this relationship comes an awareness of what to do with my life that will fulfill His calling and purpose for my existence.

One way of talking about this is to distinguish between *other-directed* and *inner-directed* living. An other-directed person looks to other people to be her compass for navigating through life. An inner-directed person has her eyes on a compass inside her, set by God.

Some of the traits of the *other-directed* person include:

- A preoccupation with what other people think of me
- A belief that I always need to *do* more for other people and God to have their approval

- A drivenness to do something so significant with my life that everyone will know of my accomplishment(s)
- An anxiety rooted in the fear of never measuring up
- Fatigue, busyness, frustration, and exasperation with the people closest to me

The traits of the *inner-directed* person are radically different:

- An enjoyment of solitude
- A sense that people are more important than projects
- An insistence on making time for celebration
- An attitude of humility and service
- A lack of urgency to have to "pin down" my calling, knowing that focusing on my Audience of One will reveal all I need to know in the right timing

Ironically, other-directedness is more selfish than inner-directedness. An inner-directed focus on Christ enables us to experience a healthy self-forgetfulness. We are no longer preoccupied with ourselves — what people think of us and how we can impress them. As inner-directed women, when we spend time with people, we are truly *with* them, not imagining how they can benefit us or help us achieve our goals. The surprising result is that we are more content and less tired. Having an Audience of One takes the stress out of life!

8. In what ways are you other-directed? In what ways are you inner-directed?

9. What is one area of your life in which you are currently challenged to please your Audience of One?

> *The chief end of any of our lives is our relationship with God. We were created to enjoy him, not primarily to serve him or to accomplish great things for him. God created us simply to be in his presence, to delight in his character and company.*
>
> —SANDRA HACKETT[2]

Pair up with a partner. Share with each other how you would like prayer for the area of your life you identified in question 9. Write a few notes if your partner agrees. Then regather as a group and pray for your partner in the area she has described.

Becoming inner-directed is a process. Nothing substitutes for seeking God alone and with others over time.

Lay before God the situation from question 9 in which you

find it hard to treat Him as your Audience. Close your eyes and listen to Jesus' words: "The one who sent me is with me; he has not left me alone, for I always do what pleases him" (John 8:29). Imagine yourself in the situation. Allow yourself to become aware of the Father with you there. What would it look like for you to please Him in the situation? Picture yourself doing that, and let yourself be aware of the Father being pleased with you. Remember that your right actions will please the Father even if other people make their own choices and the results aren't what you'd like them to be. If you have trouble imagining yourself pleasing God, go back to the verse. What part of Jesus' words do you have trouble believing for this situation?

Check in with your partner midweek to find out how her efforts to focus on her Audience of One are going. Give her the gift of honest interest in what is really happening in her life. Listen closely to her without planning a response, then pause and listen inside you to what the Holy Spirit might be giving you to say to her. Give her the genuine response of your heart, without worrying about whether it will sound spiritual enough.

> *Has anyone said it better than Oswald Chambers in his matchless description of the disciple's master passion, "My utmost for His highest"?*
>
> —Os Guinness [3]

4

DREAM GOD'S DREAMS

When God plants a dream in my heart, that becomes my purpose, my focus, and what I gather all my energies to achieve. . . . I want to live my life in such a way that when and if I grow old, I can look back and say: I did not hold back from God; I gave Him all of myself as best as I could have done. He did that and more for me.

—CHRISTINA DiSTEFANO DAVIS[1]

As a young woman in my mid-twenties, I truly desired to live out God's purpose for my life. But I kept searching for the "dot" in the center of God's will and found myself exasperated as I kept saying yes to different ministries and community activities. I would wear myself out working hard, always looking for "it"—something that felt like the fulfillment of God's dream for my life.

After four years, I left my job as a junior high English and speech teacher, but I was still looking for a *perfect* place to use my gifts. My search seemed in vain. Then one day I read a familiar verse: "Thou wilt show me the path of life: in thy presence is fullness of joy; at thy right hand there are pleasures for evermore" (Psalm 16:11, KJV).

The verse definitely indicated that God had a dream for me—the path of life. And then the light went on in my head. The way to find God's purpose for my life was to evaluate how He "wired" me—what were the things that brought me great *joy* in the process of living each day, and how did my personality, gifts, and opportunities bless the lives of others? It only made sense that the "pleasures for evermore" part of the verse meant that as God revealed His dream for my life, I would *enjoy* the process of living out the path He placed before me.

I sat down and made a random list of words or phrases that described me. Trying not to be too modest to be honest, nor too full of exaggeration to be realistic, the list looked something like this: enthusiastic, encouraging, teacher, dreamer, communicator, enjoys helping people find hope, cheerleader of others, Spirit-motivated, persuasive, creative. Evaluating each word on the list, I smiled to myself, thinking of past opportunities, events, and encounters with people when I had an opportunity to live out those descriptions. Just thinking about these things brought renewed *joy* to my heart.

Slowly I began to realize that when I dream God's dreams for my life, I need to be alert. Instead of jumping from one thing to another, it's important to evaluate each open door in the light of how God designed me. I need to ask myself, *Is this a good fit for the way He gifted me? Can I already anticipate the joy of participating in His dream through saying yes to this opportunity?*

When we're committed to follow Jesus wherever He leads, to please Him no matter what others think, and to value His call more than anything else in our lives, we're mentally prepared to receive specific guidance from Him. Now it's time to let ourselves become excited about the things that excite God. It's time to dream God's dreams.

In this session we won't try to survey all of the purposes of God laid out in the Scriptures. Instead, we'll look at three passages that sample some of God's purposes: two from the words of Jesus and one from the very beginning and foundation of the Bible. We'll also begin a three-session process of putting our own purpose into words.

1. When you were a child, what did you want to be when you grew up? (If you didn't have a clear plan, what were some of the things you liked to do?)

Understanding God's purposes in the world is a key to discerning God's call. What has God been up to all these thousands of years? It's worthwhile to read through the Bible asking that question. What does God value? What does God want done?

We will begin a very brief tour of God's purposes in Genesis 1, where we find the first instructions God gave to humans. We might call these instructions the Great Foundation because they underlie all the commandments that have come after them.

2. Read Genesis 1:26-28. This is a portion of the Creation story. What does God do in this passage?

3. What does God command humans to do in verse 28?

The words "subdue" and "rule over" in Genesis 1:28 trouble some people. Taken in isolation, these words may sound like a license to exploit the earth. In 2:15, God explains how He wants humans to exercise their authority: God puts the man into His garden "to work it and take care of it." God has given humans the responsibility to govern earth's inhabitants for the benefit of all. We don't own the earth; it is God's property, and we manage it to please Him.

Some of us resonate strongly with the Great Foundation. We recognize ourselves as people who create things because we bear the image of the Creator. We live out of a responsibility to raise families or to care for the earth and its plants and animals.

4. In what ways (if any) does Genesis 1:28 express a call you sense from God?

5. Read Matthew 22:34-40. Here Jesus states what are often called the Great Commandments. What are they?

6. How would you explain what it means to love your neighbor in the same way that you love yourself?

7. In what ways (if any) does this passage express a call you sense from God?

8. Read Matthew 28:16-20, in which Jesus gives what is known as the Great Commission. Here Jesus asserts that

the Father has given Him all authority in the universe. On the basis of this authority, He gives His followers a mission. What is that mission?

The Great Commission includes "teaching them to obey *everything* I have commanded you" (verse 19, emphasis added). "Everything" presumably includes the way of life described in the Sermon on the Mount (Matthew 5–7), the life of love we've seen in Matthew 22, and perhaps even the ministry of healing and preaching Jesus commanded the disciples to carry out (Matthew 10). "Teaching them to obey" would mean not just *telling* people to do these things but also *training* them in *how* to do them.

9. In what ways (if any) does the Great Commission express a call you sense from God?

10. God did not give us these commands to make us feel guilty and overwhelmed. He gave them to inspire us to dream His dreams. As you think about these three passages, what dreams begin to form in your heart?

Dreaming God's Dreams

As you begin to live out the dream God envisions for your future, there are specific action steps you can take. In this and the next two sessions, you'll take some steps toward putting words to your sense of God's purpose for you. A purpose statement is invaluable for setting priorities and staying focused. It needs to grow out of an ongoing commitment to discern God's dreams and follow Jesus wherever He leads.

You won't have to write a purpose statement until session 6, but to get you thinking, here are some guidelines. Your purpose statement should:

- Include both you and other people
- Include both being and doing—who you are as well as what you do
- Be stated positively (not "My purpose is to stop getting into bad relationships")
- Be something you can live out every day (not a goal you have to reach, like "make five million dollars" or "ban abortion")
- Be one sentence, and short enough that you can remember it
- Be something that *you* find very inspiring, that provides a lot of emotional juice for you

Here are some sample purpose statements:

- My purpose is to evangelize, equip, encourage, and empower people to impact others with their God-given potential. (Carol)
- My purpose is to draw myself and others into an ever-deeper experience of God's community of joy. (Karen)

- The purpose of my life is to bring out the best in myself and other people by loving, learning, leading, and living joyfully. (Cindy, a friend of ours)
- My purpose is to illuminate and inspire hurting people everywhere with the knowledge and application of God's truth. (Joy, Carol's sister)

It's important to create a purpose statement that applies not just to what we do for a living, nor just to our official "ministry," but to our entire life—including our life at a paid job, if we have one. In the examples above, Cindy seeks to work out her purpose of bringing out the best in people in her relationships, her volunteer efforts, and her career as an attorney and businessperson. Each of us has a spiritual calling and purpose, even those of us who have supposedly "secular" jobs.

There are two essential aspects of discerning your purpose. In the preceeding Bible study, you started on the first: discerning God's purposes in the world. What does God think is important? What does He want done? Your purpose will always be an aspect of His larger purposes.

The second aspect is discerning how God has made you. Questions 11 and 12 will help you start on this process. You'll do more of this in the next two sessions.

11. *Make a list of five words that describe you.* Try to be as honest as possible, omitting two extremes: false modesty and inappropriate exaggeration. If you're studying in a group, take a few minutes on your own to do this. (Here are some words that may trigger ideas for your list: inspirational, hospitable, generous, visionary, compassionate, thoughtful, joy-giver, volunteer, listener, promoter, decorator, teacher, encourager, evaluator, administrator, caregiver, intercessor, peacemaker, brightener, music-maker.)

listener encourager
administrator
sensitive

12. *What makes you weep and pound the table?* In other words, what are the causes, concerns, people groups, issues, and projects you feel deeply about—so deeply that you would be willing to invest your time, talents, and financial resources in those arenas of work or ministry? (Here are some possibilities to spark your thinking: helping children grow up wise and passionate for God, introducing others to Christ, meeting the needs of the homeless, seeking justice for the downtrodden, righting a wrong in society, organizing people, meeting the needs of the sick, loving children, caring for the brokenhearted, making the truth known, providing joyful celebrations, helping people come together in deep relationships, feeding the hungry, exposing hypocrisy, helping Christians know God more deeply, strengthening marriages, overcoming barriers between Christians and nonChristians. Think also about your ~~stopping~~ answers to questions 4, 7, 9, and 10.) ~~moral decay~~

    Take a moment to list three things you are (or could get) passionate about.

13. If you're meeting with a group, talk about what it was like to answer questions 11 and 12.

    If you couldn't come up with answers so quickly, that's okay! Many of us have trouble putting into words how we see ourselves.

Even Jesus had to go out into the wilderness to get clear about who He was and to take the full measure of His gifts. . . . He was able to describe Himself afterwards in single-word pictures . . . "I am the Light," He said. "I am the Way. I am the Vine. I am the Good Shepherd." . . . He had a multitude of powerful and positive images that communicated . . . who He was.

—LAURIE BETH JONES[2]

Offer to God your lists from questions 11 and 12. Name out loud the qualities and gifts you see in yourself, and ask God to show you how to use these to honor Him, not puff up yourself. Tell God the things you're passionate about. If you had trouble coming up with words that describe you, ask God to show you the woman He made you to be. Pray for discernment for the other members of your group. Thank God for qualities you see in them.

Go back to questions 11 and 12. Lay them before God, and take some time to listen to Him and to your heart. How would people who know you describe you? What makes you weep and pound the table? Write whatever comes to you, even if it's mixed up and vague at this point. Writing will help you untangle your thoughts. It will give you a starting point. Write a list of words or phrases, or write a stream of thoughts. Make this play, not work.

Don't rush God on this. Thank Him for giving you glimpses.

Laugh with Him about your impatience or anxiety. Remember that nobody is breathing down your neck, tapping his foot until you solve this riddle. It's not a guessing game—it's an unfolding adventure with a good God.

In session 2, it was suggested that you read a chapter of Matthew each day, asking what it reveals about God's purposes. If you've been doing that, you're halfway through Matthew by now. That reading should illuminate your purpose. If you haven't been doing that, can you start now? Or, instead of a chapter a day, you could schedule a three-hour block of time in the next week or so to get away and read all of Matthew. This may seem like a lot if your schedule is busy, but discernment takes time. It just does. And the rewards are immeasurable. Think of it as an investment in giving your life focus so you won't be busy with things that aren't central to who you are.

Other people's gifts often seem much more obvious to us than our own. Think about each woman in your small group. Maybe she found it easy to list five words that described her; maybe she found it hard. What one or two words (perhaps more) come to mind when you think of her? Write them down. Look beyond her failings to the woman God created her to be.

Send a card or e-mail to each woman, noting the words that describe her to you.

> *Our dreams are what unleash us from the dock and get us moving out on the open waters of life. Once we're in motion, the Lord steers us in directions that match the goals He has intended for us.*
>
> —DAVID J. FRAHM [3]

5

KNOW WHO
YOU AREN'T

*[God] has given each of us the gift of life with a spe-
cific purpose in view. To Him work is a sacrament,
even what we consider unimportant, mundane
work. . . . For each of us, He does have a plan. . . .
What joy to find it and even out of our helplessness,
let Him guide us in its fulfillment.*

—CATHERINE MARSHALL[1]

I slumped into my pew one Sunday morning feeling exhausted,
overworked, and used. My husband and I were in our early years
of marriage, and in addition to our full-time jobs, we were head-
ing up youth ministries at our church. Because of my background
in music, I also directed the choir and therefore produced the
Christmas and Easter cantatas as well as a choir number every
Sunday. Unexpectedly, a heavy sigh came out of my mouth.

Then I noticed Miss Giles behind me. She was a retired ele-
mentary school principal and a wise woman. She often entertained

us in her home and demonstrated her love in tangible ways. I stood up, turned around, and gave her a big hug. "Good morning, Miss Giles," I said. "It's always a joy to see you."

Her hands lingered on my shoulders. Looking deeply into my eyes, she said, "Carol, just remember, God has others."

That statement launched a change in my understanding of God's call for me. As a first-born obsessive-compulsive, workaholic, perfectionist "doer," I had taken on as many leadership roles as I could. Working harder made me feel I was doing more for God. I had never considered that by taking on so much, I was keeping other people from developing their God-given gifts.

I also realized there was sinful pride connected to the way I was carrying out God's call. I grew rather addicted to the words of other people: "Carol, you and your husband are the best youth directors we've ever had!" Or, "That choir cantata was outstanding. You are an incredible director." Or, "If you want a job done right, put Carol Kent in charge." As I thought about Miss Giles' wise words, I felt convicted. Without hurting me, Miss Giles was used by God to reveal the fact that no one *could* do everything and no one *should* do everything.

There's a powerful maturation in our lives as we discover that God's call involves discovering what He hasn't *asked* us to do and what He hasn't *gifted* us to do. And there's a burst of spiritual growth that comes when we begin helping those around us find their own calling and purpose. That often means giving them a chance to try out their gifts, knowing they might do an even better job than we could do. God asks us to dream big dreams without becoming puffed up about our own importance.

In this session we'll look at John the Baptist's humble, healthy perspective on his calling.

1. If you didn't have to work for a living, what would you like to do with the rest of your life?

Jesus said this about John the Baptist: "I tell you, among those born of women there is no one greater than John; yet the one who is least in the kingdom of God is greater than he" (Luke 7:28). John had an immense following, so huge that the Jewish leaders in Jerusalem sent officials to ask John if he regarded himself as the Messiah (John 1:19-20). People streamed from all parts of Palestine to be baptized by John. They hung on his every word. Then Jesus turned up.

2. Read John 1:19-28. How did John describe his own calling?

3. Read John 1:29-31. When John encountered Jesus, how did he compare himself with this newcomer (who happened to be his cousin)?

4. Later, Jesus began to do exactly what John was doing—baptizing people—and not far away. Read John 3:22-26. Why did this bother John's disciples?

5. Read John 3:27-30. How did John react when he learned that Jesus was taking his audience?

6. What can we learn about calling from John's reaction? Think especially about 3:27 and 3:30.

7. Do you think a celebrity speaker has more reason to feel important in the kingdom of God than a person who is called to influence only a handful of lives during her lifetime? What makes you say that?

Dreaming Freely

Knowing who we *aren't* is freeing. We don't have to push ourselves into exhaustion. We don't have to feel bad when others live out a calling that seems more glamorous than ours. We can dream big dreams without competing or comparing.

8. Take a few minutes on your own to look back over what you wrote in session 4 about yourself and your passions. Look at what you have learned about God's purposes from session 4's Bible study and from Matthew's gospel. Now answer this question: *What is your secret dream for the future?* If you could choose how you would most like to live out your purpose, what would you do?

9. If you're like most people, your inner critic immediately has a dozen reasons why your dream is absurd. What might block you from fulfilling your dream? Take a few minutes to write down your fears.

In a moment you'll get a chance to pray about your dream and offer your fears to God. As you continue to dream, keep in mind that you don't have to be the hugely successful star of a huge dream by next week. Following Christ happens one step at a time. Here are three steps to keep in mind:

- *Be observant and open to new opportunities.* At church, talking to friends, as you listen to the news or read magazines, look for ways in which your dream intersects with an opportunity.
- *Try out your idea on a small scale.* Don't think living out your purpose means you need an impressive beginning. Start small and see if God blesses your efforts and involvement.
- *Evaluate the results.* Jan Johnson says, "The best verification is to take the comments of others back to our ongoing conversation with God and ask Him to help us be discerning in our evaluation of results." [2]

In session 6, you'll have an opportunity to write a purpose statement. If you're meeting with a group, you'll want to bring all the notes you've taken about your dreams and qualities.

> *Give me a man who says this one thing I do, and not these fifty things I dabble in.*
>
> —DWIGHT L. MOODY[3]

Pair up with a partner. Tell each other your dreams, then write them down. Share briefly about your fears (don't get mired in this!).

Gather with the whole group. Offer your partner's dream to God, and ask God to give her a small-scale, first-step opportunity to try out her dream. Offer to God her fears about the things that may block her dream. Ask God that if this dream is part of His purpose for her life, He will make a way through the obstacles. Pray for courage.

Pray for your dream and your partner's dream. Continue to read Matthew and write down what you learn about God's purposes. Continue to add to your list of words that describe you.

If you're meeting with a group, remember to bring your notes from Matthew and your list of words that describe you to your meeting for session 6.

Call or e-mail your partner. Talk about what each of you is thinking about your dreams. Consider renting one of these films: *It's A Wonderful Life* or *Mr. Holland's Opus*. Watch the film together. Then go through the exercise the film suggests: What would the world be like if you had never been born? Or, what is your life's work, your "opus"? Talk about this together, even pray about it.

> *What we do on our own matters little—what counts is what God chooses to do through us.*
>
> —ELIZABETH DOLE[4]

6

LISTEN AND ACT

*There's something about turning forty that makes
me more sober than ever to the fact that I want to
live for Him, I want to die for Him. I want to live an
uncompromising life. I truly want to be a woman
that when people meet me they would believe that
Jesus existed because He was so powerful in me. I
believe that's what true Christianity is about. I fail
so much, but I want to be so filled with the river of
life that it would just splash on the people around
me. That has been my prayer. That I would just be
a true reflection of Jesus' love.*

—KATHY TROCCOLI[1]

THE decision had to be made soon. I was nearing the conclusion of
my first year of college, and it was time to declare my major. I felt I
needed to know what I was going to do with the rest of my life so
my selection of courses could be specifically directed to my future life's
work. I had the overwhelming feeling that I needed a directive from

God that would definitely tell me what my purpose in life was to be.

After praying and seeking counsel, I thought long and hard about how much I had enjoyed working with young people, especially teenagers. I knew God often gave me a "connection" with them that created an atmosphere of openness, honesty, and trust. As a teenager, I had often led the devotional part of a youth event. It seemed natural that teaching junior high and high school would be an excellent choice. This decision would mean I had found my "calling" in life.

Looking back on that decision, however, has taught me that finding our calling and purpose is a lifelong adventure. It only makes sense that our Creator would design people who can grow into His plan for their lives as they say yes to the opportunities He puts in their paths that coincide with their giftedness and with His kingdom work. It's a matter of *listening* to Him and *acting* on His leading.

In my case, I began as a public school teacher. I enjoyed the work, and my communication skills were developing at the same time. Soon I met neighbors who were interested in attending a Bible study in my home, so I used my teaching skills to share principles from the Word of God with them. Always praying for direction, I eventually got the chance to become the director of an educational program for pregnant teenagers in which I could combine my teaching background with giving wise spiritual counsel and encouragement. A move with my husband to Indiana obliged me to leave that stage of my calling and enter another. When I became a director of women's ministries, God didn't waste my background, but gave me additional opportunities to grow. And so it has gone from one year to the next as I've prayed, sought counsel, and taken one step at a time.

There was never a point in my early years when I could have

identified my "purpose statement" in one sentence, but I was always aware of God networking my path with people of influence who gave me wise counsel and with open doors for service that fit my training and passion. For most of us, God's call doesn't come once for our whole lives in a blinding vision. Discerning God's call to us is a day-by-day process of listening and acting on what we hear. In this session, we'll explore how Jesus talked about this process.

1. Who is someone who has had a positive influence in your life? How did that person influence you?

2. Do you think that person was aware of a calling to influence or care for you? What makes you say that?

Jesus taught the crowds in parables, stories designed to provoke thought. He sometimes ended with the call, "He who has ears to hear, let him hear" (Luke 8:8). This refrain was an invitation to listen, think, and respond. His disciples asked Him why He didn't speak more plainly to the crowd, and Jesus quoted the prophet Isaiah to say that those whose hearts were hard wouldn't obey even if God wrote letters in the sky. Only those who responded to the little they heard in a parable had hearts open enough to receive more truth.

3. Read Luke 8:4-15. What point was Jesus making in the parable (verses 4-8)? What response do you think He was looking for?

4. What are some of the things that keep us from hearing and responding to God's call (verses 11-15)?

5. Read Luke 8:18. Jesus says to "consider carefully how you listen" because "whoever has will be given more." What does He mean? (That is, whoever has *what* will be given more? What does this have to do with listening?)

If God gives us a small instruction and we obey it, then He will probably give us another. But if we ignore God's little assignments, should we expect to get bigger ones? Some of us want God to guide us on the big things: career, marriage, where we live, what our ministry should be. Yet if we ignore His guidance on things that seem little to us — love this person, act with integrity at the job you currently have, value time with God more than entertainment—then will He shout to get our attention on other matters?

6. "Consider carefully *how* you listen." How does a person go about listening for God's instructions?

7. Why do you suppose many people are more interested in a "capital-C" Calling than in God's daily callings?

8. Sometimes we're more focused on the things we don't know about God's call to us than we are on the things we do know. What is one (or more) thing you know God has called you to be or do at this stage of your life?

Making God's Dream for My Life a Reality
Lois Mowday Rabey says, "Living in a passionate relationship with God is not definable in words. There is no prescription one

can take to achieve the desired result. It is not a once-in-a-life-time decision to do this or that, to live this list and throw out that one. It is a journey."[2]

It's the same thing when it comes to determining your call and writing out your purpose statement. Based on what God has revealed to you at this point in your spiritual journey, you will make Spirit-led decisions to spend your time, talents, and energy on causes that line up with His purposes. However, as you grow and mature, and as you develop your spiritual giftedness, your purpose statement may need revisions. Remember, God is shaping you into a vessel of honor, and that's a *dynamic process*, not a *single event*. It means listening to His voice and acting on what you hear Him saying to you now.

9. If you're meeting with a group, pair up with a partner. Look back at session 4 and reread the "Dreaming God's Dreams" section on pages 51-53. Read the sample purpose statements out loud. Look over your notes from Matthew, your list of words that describe you, and anything you've written about your dreams. Now take five to ten minutes on your own to write out your first draft of a purpose statement for your life. Don't worry if it isn't perfect—this is your first draft.

Read your purpose statement to your partner. Talk about why you each included what you did. Revise your purpose statement if you'd like. Write out one clean copy of your purpose for yourself. Write out another copy for your partner, and write your name at the top of the paper. Give the copy to your partner.

10. Read your purpose statement to the group. Talk about what it was like for you to put your life's purpose into words. How do you see your purpose statement representing the purposes of God?

One of the unexpected benefits of living out God's dream for your life is that others take notice. Jan Johnson reminds us: "One of the best things we can contribute to the people we love is to be a woman who responds to the call of God. Through us, those we love experience the joy of following God and are often challenged to consider their own God-infused purposes."[3] They observe that when you are living out your purpose, no matter how hard the "job" is, you are enjoying the journey. They are also inspired to identify how God has designed them. Don't be surprised when they ask you for direction, resources, and hands-on help. You've just become a *woman of influence!*

> *God's purpose in guidance is not to get us to perform the right actions. His purpose is to help us become the right kind of people.*
>
> —JOHN ORTBERG[4]

Let each person pray for her partner. Use your partner's purpose statement in your prayer. If you'd like, you can simply pray, "Lord, *Name* wants to align the purpose of her life with what you think is important. Please enable her to . . . [read your partner's purpose statement here]." If anyone had trouble putting her purpose into words, that's okay—ask God to reveal her unique purpose over the coming weeks. Many (perhaps most) people need extended time and a mood of prayerful confidence in God to recognize their purpose.

Thank God for something you have gained from this group over the past six weeks.

Lay your purpose statement before God, and ask Him to show you the next step of His journey for you over the coming six months. Give yourself six months to live with this purpose statement before you rewrite it. Read it daily until you have committed it to memory. As new opportunities arise for you in the coming weeks, make a habit of asking yourself, "How does this fit with my purpose?"

Share with someone else your process of discovering God's calling to you. Share with her your purpose statement and what it has been like for you to seek clarity on this issue. Ask her what sense she has of God's purpose for her life. If she's doubtful about having a purpose, encourage her with what you see God doing in her.

> *Do you want to know the secret of the mystery of your very being and rise to become what you were born to be? Listen to Jesus of Nazareth; answer His call.*
>
> —OS GUINNESS[5]

73

NOTES

Chapter 1: *Follow Me*
1. Pam Farrel, *Woman of Influence* (Downers Grove, IL: InterVarsity, 1996), p. 11.
2. Jan Hettinga, *Follow Me* (Colorado Springs, CO: NavPress, 1996), pp. 23-24.
3. David J. Frahm, *The Great Niche Hunt* (Colorado Springs, CO: NavPress, 1991), p. 28.
4. Henry T. Blackaby and Claude V. King, *Experiencing God* (Nashville, TN: Broadman & Holman, 1994), p. 20.
5. Dee Brestin, *My Daughter, My Daughter* (Colorado Springs, CO: Chariot Victor Publishing, 1999), p. 41.
6. Christina DiStefano Davis, *Totally Surrounded* (self-published by Christina DiStefano Davis, Louisville, KY, 1998), p. 60.
7. Os Guinness, *The Call* (Nashville, TN: Word, 1998), p. 7.

Chapter 2: *Tune Out the Competition*
1. Sheila West, *Beyond Chaos* (Colorado Springs, CO: NavPress, 1991), p. 197.
2. Dee Brestin, *My Daughter, My Daughter* (Colorado Springs, CO: Chariot Victor Publishing, 1999), p. 42.
3. Pamela Muse, quoted by Dee Brestin, p. 183.
4. Dudley Lynch and Paul K. Kordis, quoted by Kevin McCarthy, *The On-Purpose Person* (Colorado Springs, CO: NavPress, 1992), p. 93.
5. Pam Farrel, *Woman of Influence* (Downers Grove, IL: InterVarsity, 1996), p. 26.

Chapter 3: *Play to an Audience of One*
1. Os Guinness, *The Call* (Nashville, TN: Word, 1998), p. 73.
2. Sandra Hackett, quoted by Lucinda Secrest McDowell, *Women's Spiritual Passages* (Wheaton, IL: Harold Shaw Publishers, 1996), pp. 198-199.
3. Guinness, p. 86.

Chapter 4: *Dream God's Dreams*
1. Christina DiStefano Davis, *Totally Surrounded* (self-published by Christina DiStefano Davis, Louisville, KY, 1998), p. 60.
2. Laurie Beth Jones, *The Path* (New York, NY: Hyperion, 1996), p. 26.
3. David J. Frahm, *The Great Niche Hunt* (Colorado Springs, CO: NavPress, 1991), p. 172.

Chapter 5: *Know Who You Aren't*
1. Catherine Marshall, quoted by Judith Couchman, *Designing a Woman's Life* (Sisters, OR: Multnomah, 1995), p. 23.
2. Jan Johnson, *Living a Purpose-Full Life* (Colorado Springs, CO: WaterBrook, 1999), p. 82.
3. Dwight L. Moody, quoted by Albert M. Wells Jr., *Inspiring Quotations* (Nashville, TN: Nelson, 1988), p. 168.
4. Elizabeth Dole, quoted in *Closer to God* (Wheaton, IL: Tyndale/Christianity Today, 1996), p. 30.

Chapter 6: *Listen and Act*

1. Kathy Troccoli, quoted by Dee Brestin, *My Daughter, My Daughter* (Colorado Springs, CO: Chariot Victor Publishing, 1999), pp. 176-177.
2. Lois Mowday Rabey, quoted by Judith Couchman, *One Holy Passion* (Colorado Springs, CO: WaterBrook, 1998), pp. 234-235.
3. Jan Johnson, *Living a Purpose-Full Life* (Colorado Springs, CO: WaterBrook, 1999), p. 186.
4. John Ortberg, *The Life You've Always Wanted* (Grand Rapids, MI: Zondervan, 1997), p. 143.
5. Os Guinness, *The Call* (Nashville, TN: Word, 1998), p. 26.

For information on scheduling Carol Kent or Karen Lee-Thorp as a speaker for your group, please contact Speak Up Speaker Services. You may call us toll free at (888) 870-7719, e-mail Speakupinc@aol.com, or visit our website at www.speakupspeakerservices.com.